COME, WALK WITH ME ...

PRAYING THE STATIONS OF THE CROSS

ARRANGED & DRAWN by
Gervase J. Duffy I.C.

MAYHEW McCRIMMON
Great Wakering

First published in Great Britain in 1983 by
MAYHEW McCRIMMON Ltd,
Great Wakering, Essex

ISBN 0 85597 330 7

Printed in Hong Kong by
Permanent Typesetting & Printing Co., Ltd.

Contents

Introduction

The Stations of the Cross are a series of meditations on the Mystery of the Passion and Death of our Lord, Jesus Christ, God made man. Traditionally there have been 14 Stations, the last of which left us with Jesus in the Tomb. I have included a 15th, the Resurrection, because I feel that the Way of the Cross makes more sense when it is seen in the light of the Resurrection. The Good News is that Jesus loves us now in all our imperfection, weakness and sinfulness, and that through Him and with Him in us, we too can rise again and walk with Him as He leads us to our Father. All we have to do is to believe in Him and trust Him and allow His love to touch us and the power of His Spirit to work for us and through us.

Jesus taught us the principles by which He lived and He invites us to do likewise. These principles we call the Beatitudes. I have included them as an introduction to the Stations because they cast fresh light on the reasons why He suffered and also why we too will be rejected by the world if we follow Him. He challenges us to live counter-culturally. He teaches us that if we wish to be really happy we have to stand within the paradox of the Beatitudes. These make sense only when we stand within them, for we find that true happiness is to be found in the Kingdom within us. We experience deep inner happiness only when we let go of the desires that attract us outwards and stand in our poverty, sharing our lives with others, witnessing to the true reality of God's power, love, truth, justice and mercy.

Mysteries cannot be solved. They can be known, however, by the one who experiences them. They are known only by our entering them. We can know the mystery of Christ's Passion, Death and Resurrection by entering it and sharing our experience, feelings and hope with Jesus. I have attempted to draw these stations in such a way as to stimulate us to enter them and then turn around and look with the eyes of faith into those of Jesus. This is 'Praying the Stations of the Cross'. If we bring all our little deaths and resurrections, which we experience daily, to Jesus and stand still in the Mystery of His suffering and listen to Him, He will shed His light on us and we will find Him in them. We will discover that He will walk with us and reveal to us through the words of Scripture, as he did to the two disciples on the road to Emmaus, the depth of His love and the joy that it brings us. I have selected a broad and flexible series of Scripture texts to enable a choice to be made by those who pray the Stations. They are intended to be used according to the needs and feelings that are being experienced by those who pray.

The Mystery of God's Providence is that in love there is pain, in suffering there is joy and that in giving we receive. As we grow in the knowledge and love of God, experiencing Him as we grow throughout our lives, we find that His love is present at every moment of our life and that we can only respond to His call at this present moment. Again and again He leads us back to the Cross; the central Mystery of our Faith.

May you experience the joy of accepting His love and discover the happiness of the Kingdom, finding yourself in Him and through Him and with Him. May He walk with you.

Grace Dieu Manor
Leicestershire

BE STILL AND KNOW THAT I AM GOD

Psalm 45: 11

Preparation

MAY the God of our Lord Jesus Christ,
the Father of Glory,
give you a spirit of wisdom and perception of what is revealed,
to bring you to full knowledge of him.

May he enlighten the eyes of your mind
so you can see what hope his call holds for you,
what rich glories he has promised the saints will inherit
and how infinitely great is the power he has exercised for us believers.

This you can tell from the strength of his power at work in Christ,
when he used it to raise him from the dead
and to make him sit at his right hand, in heaven,
far above every Sovereignty, Authority, Power or Domination,
or any other name that can be named,
not only in this age but also in the age to come.

He has put all things under his feet,
and made him, as the ruler of everything,
the head of the church;
which is his body,
the fullness of him who fills the whole creation.

Ephesians 1: 17-23

JESUS said:

I am the light of the world;
anyone who follows me will not be walking in the dark;
he will have the light of life:

John 8: 12

THIS is what he taught them:

How happy are the poor in spirit
theirs is the kingdom of heaven.

Happy the gentle:
they shall have the earth for their heritage.

Happy those who mourn:
they shall be comforted.

Happy those who hunger and thirst for what is right:
they shall be satisfied.

Happy the merciful:
they shall have mercy shown them.

Happy the pure in heart:
they shall see God.

Happy the peacemakers:
they shall be called sons of God.

Happy those who are persecuted in the cause of right:
theirs is the kingdom of heaven.

Happy are you when people abuse you and persecute you and speak all kinds of calumny against you on my account.
Rejoice and be glad, for your reward will be great in heaven.
This is how they persecuted the prophets before you.

Matthew 5: 2-12

My soul, give thanks to the Lord,
all my being, bless his holy name.
My soul, give thanks to the Lord
and never forget all his blessings.

It is he who forgives all your guilt,
who heals every one of your ills,
who redeems your life from the grave,
who crowns you with love and compassion,
who fills your life with good things,
renewing your youth like an eagle's.

The Lord does deeds of justice
gives judgement for all who are oppressed.
He made known his way to Moses
and his deeds to Israel's sons.

The Lord is compassion and love,
slow to anger and rich in mercy.
His wrath will come to an end;
he will not be angry for ever.
He does not treat us according to our sins
nor repay us according to our faults.

For as the heavens are high above the earth
so strong is his love for those who fear him;
for he knows of what we are made,
he remembers that we are dust.

Give thanks to the Lord, all his hosts,
his servants who do his will.
Give thanks to the Lord, all his works,
in every place where he rules.
My soul, give thanks to the Lord!

Psalm 102: 1-12, 14, 21-22

JESUS IS CONDEMNED TO DIE

I

FIRST STATION

Jesus is condemned to Death

Pilate said to them, 'What am I to do with Jesus who is called Christ?'
They all said, 'Let him be crucified!'
'Why?' he asked, 'What harm has he done?'
But they shouted all the louder, 'Let him be crucified!'

Then Pilate saw that he was making no impression, that in fact a riot was imminent. So he took some water, washed his hands in front of the crowd and said, 'I am innocent of this man's blood. It is your concern.'
And the people, to a man, shouted back, 'His blood be on us and on our children!'

He ordered Jesus to be first scourged and then handed over to be crucified.

Matthew 27: 22-26

The governor's soldiers took Jesus with them into the Praetorium and collected the whole cohort round him. Then they stripped him and made him wear a scarlet cloak, and having twisted some thorns into a crown they put this on to his head and placed a reed in his right hand. To make fun of him they knelt to him saying, 'Hail, King of the Jews!' And they spat on him and took the reed and struck him on the head with it. And when they had finished making fun of him, they took off the cloak and dressed him in his own clothes and led him away to crucify him.

Matthew 27: 27-31

For my part, I made no resistance
neither did I turn away.
I offered my back to those who struck me;
my cheeks to those who tore at my beard;
I did not cover my face
against insult and spittle.

Isaiah 50: 5-6

Let us wait for the virtuous man,
since he annoys us and opposes our way of life,
reproaches us for our breaches of the law
and accuses us of playing false to our upbringing.

He claims to have knowledge of God,
and calls himself a son of the Lord.
Before us he stands, a reproof to our way of thinking,
the very sight of him weighs our spirits down;
his way of life is not like other men's,
the paths he treads are unfamiliar.

In his opinion we are counterfeit;
he holds aloof from our doings as though from filth;
he proclaims the final end of the virtuous as happy
and boasts of having God for his father.

Let us see if what he says is true,
let us observe what kind of an end he himself will have.
If the virtuous man is God's son, God will take his part
and rescue him from the clutches of his enemies.

Let us test him with cruelty and with torture,
and thus explore this gentleness of his
and put his endurance to the proof.
Let us condemn him to a shameful death
since he will be looked after – we have his word for it.

Wisdom 2: 12-20

Lying witnesses arise
and accuse me unjustly.
They repay me evil for good:
my soul is forlorn.

Now that I am in trouble they gather,
they gather and mock me.
they take me by surprise and strike me
and tear me to pieces.
They provoke me with mockery on mockery
and gnash their teeth.

Psalm 34: 11-12, 15-16

It is . . . the God of our ancestors, who has glorified his servant Jesus, the same Jesus you handed over and then disowned in the presence of Pilate after Pilate had decided to release him. It was you who accused the Holy One, the Just One, you who demanded the reprieve of a murderer while you killed the Prince of Life.

God, however, raised him from the dead . . .
Now you must repent and turn to God, so that your sins may be wiped out, and so that the Lord may send the time of comfort. Then he will send you the Christ . . . that is Jesus.

Acts 3: 13-15, 20-21

In your minds you must be the same as Christ Jesus:

His state was divine,
yet he did not cling to his equality with God
but emptied himself
to assume the condition of a slave,
and became as men are;

and being as all men are,
he was humbler yet,
even to accepting death,
death on a cross.

But God raised him high
and gave him the name
which is above all other names

so that all beings
in the heavens, on earth and in the underworld,
should bend the knee at the name of Jesus
and that every tongue should acclaim
Jesus Christ as Lord,
to the glory of God the Father.

Philippians 2: 5-11

JESUS ACCEPTS HIS CROSS

II

SECOND STATION

Jesus accepts his Cross

They then took charge of Jesus, and carrying his own cross
he went out of the city to the place of the skull,
or as it was called in Hebrew, Golgotha.

John 19:17

I have come so that they may have life
and have it to the full.
I am the good shepherd:
the good shepherd is the one who lays down his life for his sheep.

The Father loves me
because I lay down my life
in order to take it up again.

No one takes it from me;
I lay it down of my own free will,

and as it is in my power to lay it down,
so it is in my power to take it up again;
and this is the command I have been given by my Father.

John 10: 10-11, 17-18

We had all gone astray like sheep,
each taking his own way,
and Yahweh burdened him
with the sins of all of us.

Harshly dealt with, he bore it humbly,
he never opened his mouth,
like a lamb that is led to the slaughter house,
like a sheep that is dumb before its shearers
never opening its mouth.

By force and by law he was taken;
would anyone plead his cause?
Yes, he was torn away from the land of the living;
for our faults struck down in death.

Isaiah 53: 6-8

Second Station

If anyone wants to be a follower of mine,
let him renounce himself and take up his cross and follow me.
For anyone who wants to save his life will lose it;
but anyone who loses his life for my sake,
and for the sake of the gospel,
will save it. Mark 8: 34-35

Have mercy on me, O Lord,
for I am in distress.
Tears have wasted my eyes,
my throat and my heart.

For my life is spent with sorrow
and my years with sighs.
Affliction has broken down my strength
and my bones waste away. Psalm 30: 10-11

The language of the cross may be illogical to those
who are not on the way to salvation, but those of us
who are on the way see it as God's power to save.
Here we are preaching a crucified Christ;
a Christ who is the power and wisdom of God.
For God's foolishness is wiser than human wisdom,
and God's weakness is stronger than human strength.
1 Corinthians 1: 18, 23-25

In the face of all my foes
I am a reproach,
an object of scorn to my neighbours
and of fear to my friends.

Those who see me in the street
run far away from me.
I am like a dead man, forgotten in men's hearts,
like a thing thrown away.

I have heard the slander of the crowd,
fear is all around me,
as they plot together against me,
as they plan to take my life. Psalm 30: 12-14

As for me, the only thing I can boast about
is the cross of our Lord Jesus Christ,
through which the world is crucified to me,
and I to the world.

Galatians 6:14

But as for me, I trust in you, Lord,
I say: 'You are my God.
My life is in your hands, deliver me
from the hands of those who hate me.

Let your face shine on your servant.
Save me in your love.'

Psalm 30: 15-17

Always, wherever we may be,
we carry with us in our body the death of Jesus,
so that the life of Jesus, too, may always be seen in our body.

2 Corinthians 4: 10

Yes, the troubles which are soon over,
though they weigh little,
train us for the carrying of a weight of eternal glory
which is out of all proportion to them.

And so we have no eyes for things that are visible,
but only for things that are invisible;
for visible things last only for a time,
and the invisible things are eternal.

2 Corinthians 4: 17-18

How great is the goodness, Lord,
that you keep for those who fear you,
that you show to those who trust you
in the sight of men.

Be strong, let your heart take courage,
all who hope in the Lord.

Psalm 30: 20, 25

THE FIRST FALL

III

THIRD STATION

The first Fall

Now the hour has come
for the Son of Man to be glorified.
I tell you, most solemnly,
unless a grain of wheat falls on the ground and dies
it remains only a single grain;
but if it dies it yields a rich harvest. John 12: 23-24

He has laid a snare underneath my feet;
he has brought me down;
he has left me deserted.

The yoke of my sins weighs down on me,
his, the hand that knotted them;
their yoke is on my neck,
he makes my energy fail.

The Lord has put me at their mercy,
I have no strength left to resist.
Lamentations 1: 13-14

Try, then, to imitate God, as children of his that he loves,
and follow Christ by loving as he loved you,
giving himself up in our place
as a fragrant offering and a sacrifice to God. Ephesians 5: 1-2

Here are we preaching a crucified Christ;
to the Jews an obstacle they cannot get over,
to the pagans madness,
but to those who have been called,
whether they are Jews or Greeks,
a Christ who is the power and wisdom of God.
For God's foolishness is wiser than human wisdom,
and God's weakness is stronger than human strength.
1 Corinthians 1: 23-25

Third Station

The serpent was the most subtle of all the wild beasts that Yahweh God had made. It asked the woman, 'Did God really say you were not to eat from any of the trees in the garden?' The woman answered the serpent, 'We may eat the fruit of the trees in the garden. But of the fruit of the tree in the middle of the garden God said, "You must not eat it, nor touch it, under pain of death".' Then the serpent said to the woman, 'No! you will not die! God knows in fact that on the day you eat it your eyes will be opened and you will be like gods, knowing good and evil.' The woman saw that the fruit was good to eat and pleasing to the eye, and that it was desirable for the knowledge that it could give. So she took some of the fruit and ate it. She gave some also to her husband who was with her and he ate it.Thenthe eyes of both of them were opened and they realised that they were naked.

Genesis 3: 1-7

Adam prefigured the one to come,
but the gift itself considerably outweighed the fall.
If it is certain that through one man's fall so many died,
it is even more certain that divine grace,
coming through the one man, Jesus Christ,
came to so many as an abundant free gift.

The results of the gift outweigh the result of one man's sin:

If it is certain that death reigned over everyone
as the consequence of one man's fall,
it is even more certain that one man, Jesus Christ,
will cause everyone to reign in life
who receives the free gift that he does not deserve,
of being made righteous.

As by one man's disobedience many were made sinners,
so by one man's obedience many will be made righteous.

Romans 5: 15-19

God dealt with sin by sending his own son in a body as physical as any sinful body, and in that body God condemned sin.

Romans 8: 3

Let us not lose sight of Jesus,
who leads us in our faith and brings it to perfection:
for the sake of the joy which was still in the future,
he endured the cross, disregarding the shamefulness of it,
and from now on has taken his place at the right of God's throne.

Think of the way he stood such opposition from sinners
and then you will not give up for want of courage.

Hebrews 12: 2-3

It was essential that he should in this way
become completely like his brothers
so that he could be a compassionate and trustworthy high priest
of God's religion, able to atone for human sins.
That is, because he has himself been through temptation
he is able to help others who are tempted.

Hebrews 2: 17-18

For though the will to do what is good is in me,
the performance is not, with the result
that instead of doing the good things I want to do,
I carry out the sinful things I do not want.
When I act against my will, then,
it is not my true self doing it,
but sin which lives in me.

What a wretched man I am!
Who will rescue me from this body doomed to death?
Thanks be to God through Jesus Christ our Lord!

Romans 7: 18-20, 24

JESUS MEETS HIS MOTHER

IV

FOURTH STATION

Jesus meets his Mother

As the child's father and mother stood there wondering at the things that were being said about him, Simeon blessed them and said to Mary his mother, 'You see this child: he is destined for the fall and for the rising of many in Israel, destined to be a sign that is rejected – and a sword will pierce your own soul too – so that the secret thoughts of many may be laid bare.'

Luke 2: 33-35

I tell you most solemnly
you will be weeping and wailing
while the world will rejoice;
You will be sorrowful
but your sorrow will turn to joy.
A woman in childbirth suffers,
because her time has come:
but when she has given birth to the child she forgets her suffering
in her joy that a man has been born into the world.
So it is with you: you are sad now,
but I shall see you again, and your hearts will be full of joy
and that joy no one shall take from you.

John 16: 20-22

All you who pass this way,
look and see:
is any sorrow like the sorrow
that afflicts me . . . ?

and that is why I weep;
my eyes dissolved in tears,
since the comforter who could revive me
is far away . . .

Lamentations 1: 12, 16

How can I describe you, to what compare you,
daughter of Jerusalem?
Who can rescue and comfort you,
virgin daughter of Zion?
For huge as the sea is your affliction;
who can possibly cure you?

Lamentations 2: 13

My spirit fails
my heart is numb within me.

I remember the days that are past:
I ponder on all your works.
I muse on what your hand has wrought
and to you I stretch out my hands.

In the morning let me know your love
for I put my trust in you.
Make me know the way I should walk:
to you I lift up my soul.

Rescue me, Lord, from my enemies;
I have fled to you for refuge.
Teach me to do your will
for you, O Lord, are my God.

Psalm 142: 4-6, 8-10

For I am certain of this:
neither death, nor life, no angel, no prince,
nothing that exists, nothing still to come,
not any power, or height or depth, nor any created thing,
can ever come between us
and the love of God made visible in Christ Jesus our Lord.

Romans 8: 38-39

My dear people, let us love one another since love comes from God and everyone who loves is begotten by God and knows God. Anyone who fails to love can never have known God, because God is love. God's love for us was revealed when God sent into the world his only Son so that we may have life through him. 1 John 4: 7-9

You are to conceive and bear a son,
and you must name him Jesus.
He will be great and will be called Son of the Most High.
The Lord God will give him the throne of his ancestor David;
he will rule over the House of Jacob for ever
and his reign will have no end.

The Holy Spirit will come upon you
and the power of the Most High will cover you with its shadow.
And so the child will be holy and will be called Son of God.

'I am the handmaid of the Lord,' said Mary
'let what you have said be done to me.'

Luke 1: 32, 33, 35, 38

My soul glorifies the Lord,
my spirit rejoices in God my saviour.
He looks on his servant in her lowliness;
henceforth all ages will call me blessed.

The Almighty works marvels for me.
Holy his name!
His mercy is from age to age,
on those who fear him.

He puts forth his arm in strength
and scatters the proud-hearted.
He casts the mighty from their thrones
and raises the lowly.

He fills the starving with good things,
sends the rich away empty.

He protects Israel, his servant,
remembering his mercy,
the mercy promised to our fathers,
to Abraham and his sons for ever.

Luke 1: 46-55

SIMON OF CYRENE HELPS JESUS CARRY THE CROSS

FIFTH STATION

Simon of Cyrene helps Jesus carry the Cross

As they were leading him away they seized on a man,
Simon from Cyrene, who was coming in from the country,
and made him shoulder the cross and carry it behind Jesus.

Luke 23: 26

If anyone wants to be a follower of mine,
let him renounce himself
and take up his cross every day and follow me.

For anyone who wants to save his life will lose it:
but anyone who loses his life for my sake,
that man will save it.

Luke 9: 23-24

Anyone who does not carry his cross and come after me
cannot be my disciple.

Luke 14: 27

Anyone who loves his life loses it;
anyone who hates his life in this world
will keep it for the eternal life.
If a man serves me, he must follow me,
wherever I am, my servant will be there too.
If anyone serves me, my Father will honour him.

John 12: 25-26

Come to me, all you who labour and are overburdened,
and I will give you rest.
Shoulder my yoke and learn from me,
for I am gentle and humble in heart,
and you will find rest for your souls.
Yes, my yoke is easy and my burden light.

Matthew 11: 28-30

I am the Way, the Truth and the Life.
No one can come to the Father except through me.

John 14: 6

Happy are you when people hate you,
drive you out, abuse you,
denounce your name as criminal,
on account of the Son of Man.

Rejoice when that day comes and dance for joy,
for then your reward will be great in heaven.

This was the way their ancestors treated the prophets.

Luke 6: 22-23

There is nothing I cannot master
with the help of the One who gives me strength.

Philippians 4: 13

And so Jesus too suffered outside the gate to sanctify the people with his own blood. Let us go to him, then, outside the camp, and share his degradation. For there is no eternal city for us in this life but we look for one in the life to come. Through him, let us offer God an unending sacrifice of praise, a verbal sacrifice that is offered every time we acknowledge his name. Keep doing good works and sharing your resources, for these are sacrifices that please God.

Hebrews 13: 12-16

The disciple is not superior to his teacher,
nor the slave to his master.
It is enough for the disciple
that he should grow to be like his teacher,
and the slave like his master.

If they have called the master of the house Beelzebul,
what will they not say of his household?

Matthew 10: 24-25

Slaves must be respectful and obedient to their masters, not only when they are kind and gentle but also when they are unfair. You see, there is some merit in putting up with the pains of unearned punishment if it is done for the sake of God but there is nothing meritorious in taking a beating patiently if you have done something wrong to deserve it. The merit, in the sight of God, is bearing it patiently when you are punished after doing your duty.

This, in fact, is what you were called to do, because Christ suffered for you and left an example for you to follow the way he took.

1 Peter 2: 18-21

No one can hurt you if you are determined to do only what is right: if you do have to suffer for being good, you will count it a blessing. There is no need to be afraid or to worry about them. Simply reverence the Lord Christ in your hearts, and always have an answer ready for people who ask you the reason for the hope that you all have. But give it with courtesy and respect and with a clear conscience, so that those who slander you when you are living a good life in Christ may be proved wrong in the accusations that they bring. And if it is the will of God that you should suffer, it is better to suffer for doing right than for doing wrong.

1 Peter 3: 13-17

If you can have some share in the sufferings of Christ, be glad, because you will enjoy a much greater gladness when his glory is revealed. It is a blessing for you when they insult you for bearing the name of Christ, because it means that you have the Spirit of glory, the Spirit of God resting on you . . . If anyone of you should suffer for being a Christian, then he is not to be ashamed of it; he should thank God that he has been called one.

1 Peter 4: 13-16

Remember the words I said to you:
A servant is not greater than his master.
If they persecuted me,
they will persecute you too.

John 15: 20

VERONICA WIPES THE FACE OF JESUS

VI

SIXTH STATION

Veronica wipes the face of Jesus

Without beauty, without majesty (we saw him),
no looks to attract our eyes;

a thing despised and rejected by men,
a man of sorrows and familiar with suffering,
a man to make people screen their faces;
he was despised and we took no account of him.

And yet ours were the sufferings he bore,
ours the sorrows he carried.

But we, we thought of him as someone punished,
struck by God, and brought low.

Yet he was pierced through for our faults,
crushed for our sins.
On him lies a punishment that brings us peace,
and through his wounds we are healed.

Isaiah 53: 2-5

But I am a worm and no man,
the butt of men, laughing-stock of the people.
All who see me deride me.
They curl their lips, they toss their heads.
'He trusted in the Lord, let him save him;
let him release him if he is his friend.'

Psalm 21: 7-9

Come you whom my Father has blessed –

I was hungry and you gave me food; I was thirsty and you gave me drink;
I was a stranger and you made me welcome;
naked and you clothed me, sick and you visited me,
in prison and you came to see me.

In so far as you did this to one of the least of these brothers of mine, you did it to me.

Matthew 25: 34-37, 40

Blessed be the God and Father of our Lord Jesus Christ,
a gentle Father and the Lord of all consolation,
who comforts us in all our sorrows,
so that we can offer others,
in their sorrows,
the consolation we have received from God ourselves.

Indeed as the sufferings of Christ overflow to us,
so, through Christ does our consolation overflow.

2 Corinthians 1: 3-5

Stretch your hand out also to the poor man,
that your blessing may be perfect.
Be generous in your gifts to all the living,
do not withold your favour even from the dead.

Do not fail those who weep,
but share the grief of the grief-stricken.
Do not shrink from visiting the sick;
in this way you will make yourself loved.

In everything you do remember your end,
and you will never sin.

Ecclesiasticus 7: 32-36

Bless those who persecute you: never curse them, bless them.
Rejoice with those who rejoice and be sad with those in sorrow.
Treat everyone with equal kindness;
never be condescending but make real friends with the poor.
Do not allow yourselves to become self-satisfied . . .
Do all you can to live at peace with everyone.
Never try to get revenge.

Romans 12: 14-19

It is not easy to die
even for a good man
– though, of course, for someone really worthy,
a man might be prepared to die –
but what really proves that God loves us
is that Christ died for us while we were still sinners.

Romans 5: 7-8

This befell us though we had not forgotten you;
though we had not been false to your covenant,
though we had not withdrawn our hearts;
though our feet had not strayed from your path.

Yet you have crushed us in a place of sorrows
and covered us with the shadow of death.

Psalm 43: 18-20

In you, O lord, I take refuge;
let me never be put to shame.
In your justice rescue me, free me:
Pay heed to me and save me.

Be a rock where I can take refuge,
a mighty stronghold to save me;
for you are my rock, my stronghold.

My fate has filled many with awe
but you are my strong refuge.

For my enemies are speaking about me;
those who watch me take counsel together
saying: 'God has forsaken him; follow him,
seize him; there is no one to save him.'

O God, do not stay far off:
my God, make haste to help me!

Psalm 70: 1-3, 7, 10-12

I will declare the Lord's mighty deeds
proclaiming your justice, yours alone.
O God, you have taught me from my youth
and I proclaim your wonders still.

You have burdened me with bitter troubles
but you will give me back my life.
You will raise me from the depths of the earth;
you will exalt me and console me again.

Psalm 70: 16-17, 20-21

THE SECOND FALL

VII

SEVENTH STATION

The second Fall

My enemies whisper together against me.
They all weigh up the evil which is on me:
'Some deadly thing has fastened upon him,
he will not rise again from where he lies.'
Thus even my friend, in whom I trusted,
who ate my bread, has turned against me.

Psalm 40: 8-10

Peter was sitting outside in the courtyard, and a servant-girl came up to him and said, 'You too were with Jesus the Galilean'. But he denied it in front of them all. 'I do not know what you are talking about,' he said. When he went out to the gateway another servant-girl saw him and said to the people there, 'This man was with Jesus the Nazarene'. And again with an oath, he denied it, 'I do not know the man'. A little later the bystanders came up and said to Peter, 'You are one of them for sure! Why, your accent gives you away.' Then he started calling down curses on himself and swearing, 'I do not know the man'. At that moment the cock crew, and Peter remembered what Jesus had said, 'Before the cock crows you will have disowned me three times'. And he went outside and wept bitterly.

Matthew 26: 69-75

But you, O Lord, have mercy on me.
Let me rise once more and I will repay them.
By this shall I know that you are my friend,
if my foes do not shout in triumph over me.
If you uphold me I shall be unharmed
and set in your presence for evermore.

Psalm 40: 11-13

O God, hear my cry! Listen to my prayer!
From the end of the earth I call; my heart is faint.

Let me dwell in your tent for ever
and hide in the shelter of your wings.

Psalm 60: 2, 3, 5

Save me, O God for the waters have risen to my neck.

I have sunk into the mud of the deep and there is no foothold.
I haver entered the waters of the deep
and the waves overwhelm me.

Psalm 68: 2, 3

When the disciples saw him walking on the lake they were terrified. 'It is a ghost,' they said, and cried out in fear. But at once Jesus called out to them, saying, 'Courage! It is I! Do not be afraid.' It was Peter who answered. 'Lord,' he said, 'if it is you, tell me to come to you across the water.' 'Come,' said Jesus. Then Peter got out of the boat and started walking towards Jesus across the water, but as soon as he felt the force of the wind, he took fright and began to sink. 'Lord! Save me!' he cried. Jesus put out his hand at once and held him. 'Man of little faith,' he said 'why did you doubt?' And as they got into the boat the wind dropped.

Matthew 14: 26-32

I am wearied with all my crying
my throat is parched.
My eyes are wasted away
from looking for my God.

Psalm 68: 4

Mary of Magdala . . . came running to Simon Peter and the other disciple, the one Jesus loved. 'They have taken the Lord out of the tomb,' she said 'and we don't know where they have put him.' So Peter set out with the other disciple to go to the tomb. They ran together . . . Simon Peter . . . - went right into the tomb, saw the linen cloths on the ground, and also the cloth that had been over his head . . . The disciples then went home again.

John 20: 2, 3, 6, 10

Why do you hide your face
and forget our oppression and misery?
For we are brought down low to the dust;
our body lies prostrate on the earth;
Stand up and come to our help!
Redeem us because of your love!

Psalm 43: 25-27

Jesus said to Simon Peter, 'Simon son of John, do you love me more than these others do?' He answered, 'Yes Lord, you know I love you'. Jesus said to him, 'Feed my lambs'. A second time he said to him, 'Simon son of John, do you love me?' He replied, 'Yes, Lord, you know I love you'. Jesus said to him, 'Look after my sheep'. Then he said to him a third time, 'Simon son of John, do you love me?' Peter was upset that he asked him the third time, 'Do you love me?' and said, 'Lord you know everything; You know I love you'. Jesus said to him 'Feed my sheep' . . . After this he said, 'Follow me'.

John 21: 15-17, 19

Lord, let my cry come before you:
teach me by your word.
Let my pleading come before you:
save me by your promise.

Let my lips proclaim your praise
because you teach me your statutes.
Let my tongue sing your promise
for your commands are just.
Let your hand be ready to help me,
since I have chosen your precepts.

Lord, I long for your saving help
and your law is my delight.
Give life to my soul that I may praise you.
Let your decrees give me help.

I am lost like a sheep; seek your servant
for I remember your commands.

Psalm 118: 169-176

I have become an object of scorn
all who see me toss their heads.

Help me, Lord my God;
save me because of your love.
Let them know that this is your work,
that this is your doing, O Lord.

Psalm 108: 25-27

JESUS SPEAKS TO THE WOMEN OF JERUSALEM

EIGHTH STATION

Jesus speaks to the Women of Jerusalem

Large numbers of people followed him, and of women too, who mourned and lamented for him. But Jesus turned to them and said, 'Daughters of Jerusalem, do not weep for me; weep rather for yourselves and for your children. For the days will surely come when people will say, "Happy are those who are barren, the wombs that have never borne, the breasts that have never suckled!" Then they will begin to say to the mountains, "Fall on us!"; to the hills "Cover us!" For if men use the green wood like this, what will happen when it is dry?'

Luke 23: 27-31

As he drew near and came in sight of the city he shed tears over it and said, 'If you in your turn had only understood on this day the message of peace! But, alas, it is hidden from your eyes! Yes, a time is coming when your enemies will raise fortifications all round you, when they will encircle you and hem you in on every side; they will dash you and the children inside your walls to the ground; they will leave not one stone standing on another within you – and all because you did not recognise your opportunity when God offered it!'

Luke 19: 41-44

'Jerusalem, Jerusalem, you that kill the prophets and stone those who are sent to you! How often have I longed to gather your children, as a hen gathers her chicks under her wings, and you refused! So be it! Your house will be left to you desolate, for, I promise, you shall not see me any more until you say: "Blessings on him who comes in the name of the Lord!" '

Matthew 23: 37-39

'Where did the man get this wisdom and these miraculous powers? This is the carpenter's son surely? . . . So where did the man get it all?' And they would not accept him. But Jesus said to them, 'A prophet is only despised in his own country and in his own house.'

Matthew 13: 54-57

Israel was a luxuriant vine
yielding plenty of fruit.
The more his fruit increased,
the more altars he built;

the richer his land became,
the richer he made the sacred stones.

Their heart is a divided heart;
very well, they must pay for it:
Yahweh is going to break their altars down
and destroy their sacred stones.

Hosea 10: 1-2

You must not love this passing world
or anything that is in the world.

The love of the Father cannot be
in any man who loves the world,
because nothing the world has to offer
– the sensual body,
the lustful eye,
pride in possessions –
could ever come from the Father
but only from the world;

and the world, with all it craves for,
is coming to an end;
but anyone who does the will of God
remains for ever.

1 John 2: 15-17

He was in the world
that had its being through him,
and the world did not know him.
He came to his own domain
and his own people did not accept him.
But to all who did accept him
he gave power to become children of God.

John 1: 10-12

Whoever believes in me
believes not in me but in the one who sent me,

and whoever sees me, sees the one who sent me.

I, the light, have come into the world
so that whoever believes in me
need not stay in the dark any more.

John 12: 44-46

You are sad now, but I shall see you again,
and your hearts will be full of joy, and that joy no one shall take from you.

John 16: 22

We can be sure that we are in God
only when the one who claims to be living in him
is living the same kind of life as Christ lived.

1 John 2: 5

Our love is not to be just words or mere talk,
but something real and active;
only by this can we be certain that we are children of the truth.

1 John 3: 18

Yahweh, remember what has happened to us;
look on and see our degradation.

Our fathers have sinned; they are no more,
and we ourselves bear the weight of their crimes.

Joy has vanished from our hearts;
our dancing has been turned to mourning.

But you, Yahweh, you remain for ever;
your throne endures from age to age.

You cannot mean to forget us for ever?
You cannot mean to abandon us for good?

Make us come back to you, Yahweh, and we will come back.
Renew our days as in times past.

Lamentations 5: 1, 7, 15, 19-21

THE THIRD FALL
IX

NINTH STATION

The third Fall

I am bowed and brought to my knees.

Spent and utterly crushed,
I cry aloud in anguish of heart.

O Lord, you know my longing:
my groans are not hidden from you.
My heart throbs, my strength is spent;
the very light has gone from my eyes.

Psalm 37: 7, 9-11

He had not done anything wrong,
and there had been no perjury in his mouth.
He was insulted and did not retaliate with insults;
when he was tortured he made no threats
but he put his trust in the righteous judge.
He was bearing our faults in his own body on the cross,
so that we might die to our faults
and live for holiness;
through his wounds you have been healed.

1 Peter 2: 22-24

Lord, answer, for your love is kind;
in your compassion, turn towards me.
Do not hide your face from your servant.

Taunts have broken my heart;
I have reached the end of my strength.

As for me in my poverty and pain
Let your help, O God, lift me up.

Psalm 68: 17, 18, 21, 30

He was crucified through weakness, and still he lives now through the power of God. So, then, we are weak, as he was, but we shall live with him, through the power of God.

2 Corinthians 13: 4

My friends avoid me like a leper;
those closest to me stand afar off.
For I am on the point of falling
and my pain is always before me.

O Lord, do not forsake me!
My God, do not stay afar off!
Make haste and come to my help,
O Lord, my God, my Saviour.

Psalm 37: 12, 18, 22, 23

During his life on earth,
he offered up prayer and entreaty,
aloud and in silent tears,
to the one who had the power to save him out of death,
and he submitted so humbly that his prayer was heard.

Although he was Son,
he learnt to obey through suffering;
but having been made perfect,
he became for all who obey him
the source of eternal salvation.

Hebrews 5: 7-9

Yahweh has been pleased to crush him with suffering.
If he offers his life in atonement . . .
through him what Yahweh wishes will be done . . .

By his sufferings my servant will justify many,
taking their faults on himself . . .

bearing the faults of many
and praying all the time for sinners.

Isaiah 53: 10-12

Happy those who are persecuted in the cause of right:
theirs is the kingdom of heaven.
Happy are you when people abuse you and speak all kinds of calumny against you on my account. Rejoice and be glad, for your reward will be great in heaven. This is how they persecuted the prophets before you.

Matthew 5: 10-12

We are in difficulties on all sides, but never cornered:
we see no answer to our problems, but never despair:

we have been persecuted, but never deserted;
knocked down, but never killed:

always, wherever we may be,
we carry with us in our body the death of Jesus,
so that the life of Jesus, too, may always be seen in our body.

2 Corinthians 4: 8-10

If you belonged to the world
the world would love you as its own;

but because you do not belong to the world,
because my choice withdrew you from the world,
therefore the world hates you.

Remember the words I said to you:
a servant is not greater than his master.
If they persecuted me,
they will persecute you too.

John 15: 18-20

The proud have risen against me;
ruthless men seek my life:
to you they pay no heed.

Psalm 85: 14

More numerous than the hairs on my head
are those who hate me without cause.
Those who attack me with lies
are too much for my strength.

Psalm 68: 5

He has said, 'My grace is enough for you: my power is at its best in weakness'. So . . . I am quite content with my weaknesses, and with insults, hardships . . . and the agonies I go though for Christ's sake. For it is when I am weak that I am strong.

2 Corinthians 12: 9, 10

JESUS IS STRIPPED

X

TENTH STATION

Jesus is stripped

When the soldiers had finished crucifying Jesus they took his clothing and divided it into four shares, one for each soldier. His undergarment was seamless, woven in one piece from neck to hem; so they said to one another, 'Instead of tearing it, let's throw dice to decide who is to have it'.

John 19: 24

Parched as burnt clay is my throat
my tongue cleaves to my jaws.

I can count every one of my bones.
These people stare at me and gloat;
they divide my clothing among them.
They cast lots for my robe.

Psalm 21: 16, 18, 19

Why are your garments red,
your clothes as if you had trodden the winepress?

I have trodden the winepress alone.
Of the men of my people not one was with me.
I looked: there was no one to help;
not one could I find to support me.

Isaiah 63: 2, 3, 5

I exult for joy in Yahweh,
my soul rejoices in my God,
for he has clothed me in the garments of salvation,
he has wrapped me in the cloak of integrity,
like a bridegroom wearing his wreath
like a bride adorned in her jewels.

Isaiah 61: 10

Blessed are the poor in spirit,
theirs is the kingdom of heaven.

Matthew 5: 3

Remember how generous the Lord Jesus was:
he was rich, but he became poor for your sake,
to make you rich out of his poverty.

2 Corinthians 8: 9

The time came for her to have her child, and she gave birth to a son, her first-born. She wrapped him in swaddling clothes, and laid him in a manger because there was no room for them at the inn.

Luke 2: 6-8

'If you wish to be perfect, go and sell what you own and give the money to the poor, and you will have treasure in heaven; then come, follow me.'

Matthew 19: 21

We brought nothing into the world, and we can take nothing out of it.

1 Timothy 6: 7

You see, God's grace has been revealed, and it has made salvation possible for the whole human race, and taught us that what we have to do is to give up everything that does not lead to God, and all our human ambitions . . .

He sacrificed himself for us in order to set us free from all wickedness and to purify a people so that it could be his very own and would have no ambition except to do good.

Titus 2: 11-14

God has imprisoned all men in their own disobedience
only to show mercy to all mankind.

Romans 11: 32

You must kill everything in you that belongs only to earthly life.
You have stripped off your old behaviour with your old self,
and have put on a new self
which will progress towards true knowledge
the more it is renewed in the image of its creator;
and in that image . . . there is only Christ:
he is everything and he is in everything.

Colossians 3: 5, 10, 11

I am the one he has driven and forced to walk
in darkness, and without any light.
He has wasted my flesh and skin away,
has broken my bones.
He has made a yoke for me,
has encircled my head with weariness.
He has filled my paths with briars and torn me,
he has made me a thing of horror.

Lamentations 3: 2, 4, 5, 11

'My portion is Yahweh' says my soul
'and so I will hope in him'.
Yahweh is good to those who trust him,
to the soul that searches for him.

Lamentations 3: 24, 25

JESUS IS NAILED TO THE CROSS

ELEVENTH STATION

Jesus is nailed to the Cross

Many dogs have surrounded me,
a band of the wicked beset me.
They tear holes in my hands and my feet
and lay me in the dust of death.

Psalm 21: 17

A man can have no greater love
than to lay down his life for his friends.
You are my friends,
if you do what I command you.

John 15: 13

He has cancelled every record of the debt that we had to pay: he has done away with it by nailing it to the cross.

Colossians 2: 14

The marks on my body are those of Jesus.

Galatians 6: 17

If anyone asks him 'Then what are these wounds on your body?' he will reply, 'These I received in the house of my friends.'

Zechariah 13: 6

If I were to seek my own glory that would be no glory at all:
my glory is conferred by the Father.

John 8: 54

By his sufferings shall my servant justify many,
taking their faults on himself . . .
by surrendering himself to death
and letting himself be taken for a sinner,
while he was bearing the faults of many
and praying all the time for sinners.

Isaiah 53: 11-12

Eleventh Station

When they reached the place called The Skull, they crucified him there and the two criminals also, one on the right, the other on the left. Jesus said, 'Father, forgive them; they do not know what they are doing'.
One of the criminals hanging there abused him. 'Are you not the Christ?' he said. 'Save yourself and us as well.' But the other spoke up and rebuked him. 'Have you no fear of God at all?' he said. 'You got the same sentence as he did, but in our case we deserved it: we are paying for what we did. But this man has done nothing wrong. Jesus,' he said 'remember me when you come into your kingdom.' 'Indeed, I promise you,' he replied 'today you will be with me in paradise.'

Luke 23: 33-34, 39-43

God's love for us was revealed
when God sent into the world his only Son
so that we could have life from him;
this is the love I mean:
not our love for God,
but God's love for us when he sent his Son
to be the sacrifice that takes our sins away.

1 John 4: 9-10

Now sentence is being passed on this world;
now the prince of this world is to be overthrown
and when I am lifted up from the earth,
I shall draw all men to myself.

John 12: 31-32

The life and death of each one of us has an influence on others; if we live, we live for the Lord; and if we die, we die for the Lord, so that alive or dead we belong to the Lord . . . This is why you should never pass judgement on a brother or treat him with contempt . . . It is to God that each one of us must give an account of himself.

Romans 14: 7, 8, 10, 12

To suffer in God's way means changing for the better and leaves no regrets, but to suffer as the world knows suffering brings death.

2 Corinthians 7: 10

God sent fiery serpents among the people; their bite brought death to many in Israel. The people came and said to Moses, 'We have sinned by speaking against Yahweh and against you. Intercede for us with Yahweh to save us from these serpents.' Moses interceded for the people, and Yahweh answered him, 'Make a fiery serpent and put it on a standard. If anyone is bitten and looks at it, he shall live.' So Moses fashioned a bronze serpent which he put on a standard, and if anyone was bitten by a serpent, he looked at the bronze serpent and lived.

Numbers 21: 6-9

What shall I say?
Father, save me from this hour?
But it was for this reason that I have come to this hour.
Father, glorify your name!

John 12: 27

Father, the hour has come:
glorify your Son
so that your Son may glorify you;
and through the power over all mankind that you have given him,
let him give eternal life to all those you have entrusted to him.
And eternal life is this:
to know you, the only true God
and Jesus Christ whom you have sent.

John 17: 1-3

What the Spirit brings is very different: love, joy, peace, patience, kindness, goodness, trustfulness, gentleness and self-control. You cannot belong to Jesus Christ unless you crucify all self-indulgent passions and desires.

Galatians 5: 22-24

INRI

JESUS DIES ON THE CROSS

XII

TWELFTH STATION

Jesus dies on the Cross

From the sixth hour there was darkness over all the land until the ninth hour.

Matthew 27: 45

And at the ninth hour Jesus cried out in a loud voice 'Eloi, Eloi, lama sabachthani?' which means 'My God, my God why have you deserted me?'

Mark 15: 33-34

When Jesus had cried out in a loud voice, he said, 'Father into your hands I commend my spirit.'

Luke 23: 46

Jesus knew that everything had now been completed, and to fulfill the scripture perfectly he said, 'I am thirsty'. A jar full of vinegar stood there, so putting a sponge soaked in the vinegar on a hyssop stick they held it up to his mouth. After Jesus had taken the vinegar he said, 'It is accomplished': and bowing his head he gave up his spirit.

John 19: 28-30

My God, my God, why have you forsaken me?
You are far from my plea and the cry of my distress.

All who see me deride me.
They curl their lips, they toss their heads.
'He trusted in the Lord, let him save him:
Let him release him if this is his friend'.

Psalm 21: 2, 8, 9

The passers-by jeered at him: they shook their heads and said, 'So you would destroy the Temple and rebuild it in three days! Then save yourself! If you are God's son, come down from the cross!' The chief priests with the scribes and elders mocked him in the same way. 'He saved others;' they said, 'he cannot save himself. He is the king of Israel; let him come down from the cross now, and we will believe in him. He put his trust in God: now let God rescue him if he wants him. For he did say "I am the son of God".'

Matthew 27: 39-43

See my servant will prosper,
he shall be lifted up, exalted, rise to great heights.

As the crowds were appalled on seeing him
 – so disfigured did he look
 that he seemed no longer human –
so will the crowds be astonished at him.
and kings stand speechless before him;
For they shall see something never told
and witness something never heard before:

'Who could believe what we have heard
and to whom has the power of Yahweh been revealed?'
Like a sapling he grew up in front of us
like a root in arid ground.

Isaiah 52: 13-15; 53: 1-2

Near the cross of Jesus stood his mother and his mother's sister, Mary the wife of Clopas, and Mary of Magdala. Seeing his mother and the disciple he loved standing near her, Jesus said to his mother, 'Woman this is your son'. Then to the disciple he said, 'This is your mother'. And from that moment the disciple made a place for her in his home.

John 19: 25-27

My little children, I shall not be with you much longer.
You will look for me,
and, as I told the Jews, where I am going, you cannot come.
I give you a new commandment:
love one another;
just as I have loved you, you must also love one another.
By this love you have for one another,
everyone will know that you are my disciples.

John 13: 33-35

Now sentence is being passed on this world;
now the prince of this world is to be overthrown.
And when I am lifted up from the earth,
I shall draw all men to myself.

John 12: 31-32

The Son of Man must be lifted up
as Moses lifted up the serpent in the desert,
so that everyone who believes may have eternal life in him.
Yes, God loved the world so much
that he gave his only son,
so that everyone who believes in him may not be lost
but may have eternal life.

John 3: 13-16

A man can have no greater love than to lay down his life for his friends.
You are my friends if you do what I command you . . .
I call you friends, because I have made known to you
everything I have learnt from my Father . . .
What I command you is to love one another.

John 15: 13, 14, 17

His state was divine,
yet he did not cling to his equality with God
but emptied himself to assume the condition of a slave,
and became as men are;
and being as all men are, he was humbler yet,
even to accepting death, death on a cross.

Philippians 2: 6-8

For anyone who is in Christ,
there is a new creation . . .
It is all God's work.

It was God who reconciled us to himself through Christ . . .
God in Christ was reconciling the world to himself,
not holding men's faults against them . . .
be reconciled to God . . .

For our sake God made the sinless one into sin,
so that in him we might become the goodness of God.

Now is the favourable time,
this is the day of salvation.

2 Corinthians 5: 17-19, 21; 6: 2

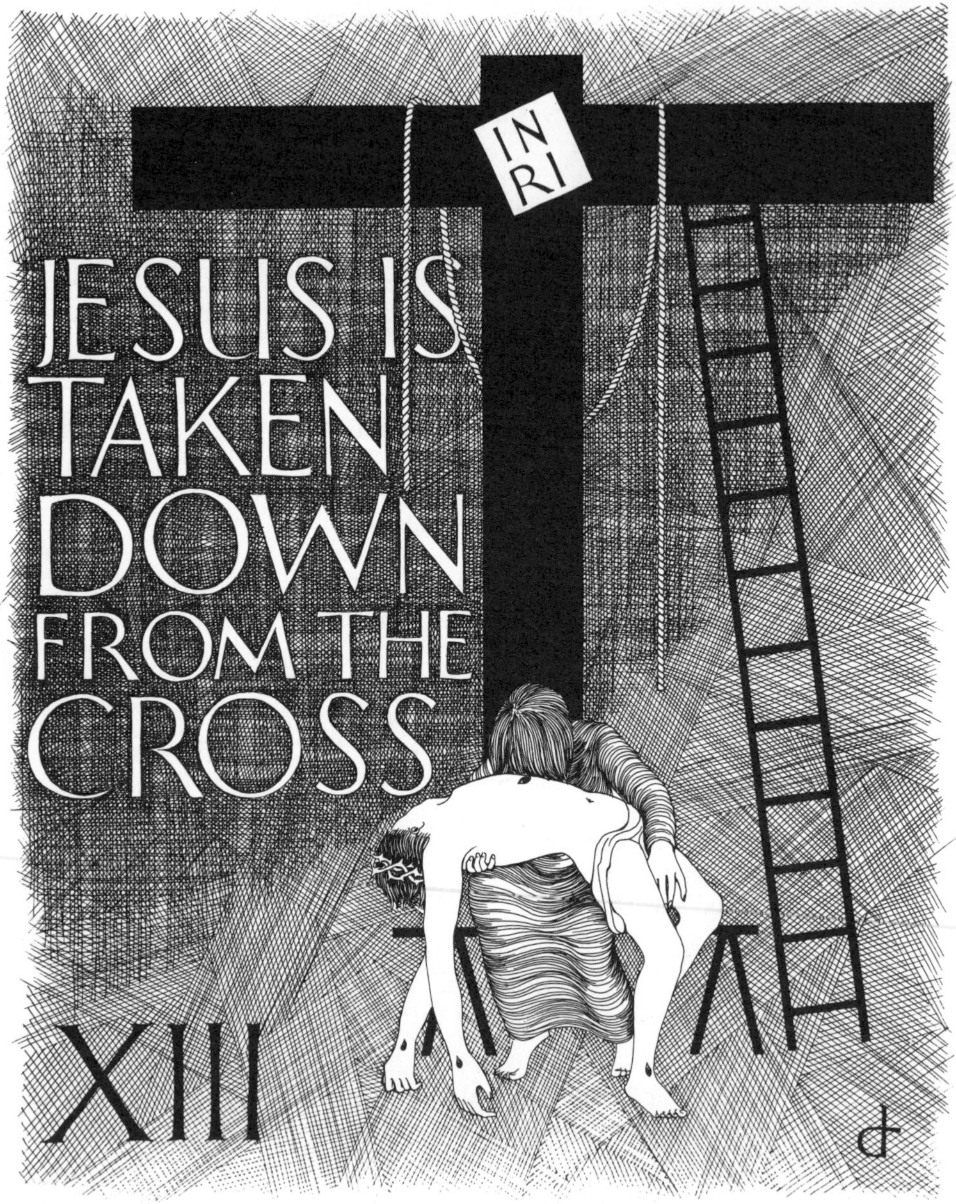

INRI

JESUS IS TAKEN DOWN FROM THE CROSS

XIII

THIRTEENTH STATION

Jesus is taken down from the Cross

The soldiers came and broke the legs of the first man who had been crucified with him and then of the other. When they came to Jesus, they found he was already dead, and so instead of breaking his legs one of the soldiers pierced his side with a lance; and immediately there came out blood and water.

After this, Joseph of Arimathea, who was a disciple of Jesus – though a secret one because he was afraid of the Jews – asked Pilate to let him remove the body of Jesus. Pilate gave permission. John 19: 32-34, 38

Jesus Christ, the faithful witness, the First-born from the dead, the Ruler of the kings of the earth. He loves us and has washed away our sins with his blood and made us a line of kings, priests to serve his God and Father: to him, then, be glory and power for ever and ever. Amen.

It is he who is coming on the clouds; everyone will see him, even those who pierced him, and all the races of the earth will mourn over him. This is the truth. Amen.

Revelation 1: 5-7

Oh, come to the water all you who are thirsty;
though you have no money, come!
Buy corn without money, and eat,
and, at no cost, wine and milk.
Why spend money on what is not bread,
your wages on what fails to satisfy?
Listen, listen to me, and you will have good things to eat
and rich food to enjoy.
Pay attention, come to me;
listen, and your soul will live.

Isaiah 55: 1-3

I am the bread of life.
He who comes to me will never be hungry;
he who believes in me will never thirst.

John 6: 35

Let the wicked man abandon his way,
the evil man his thoughts.
Let him turn back to Yahweh who will take pity on him,
to our God who is rich in forgiving;

for my thoughts are not your thoughts,
my ways not your ways – it is Yahweh who speaks.
Yes, the heavens are as high above the earth
as my ways are above your ways,
my thoughts above your thoughts.

Isaiah 55: 7-9

It is the spirit that gives life,
the flesh has nothing to offer.
The words I have spoken to you are spirit
and they are life.

John 6: 62-63

Everyone moved by the Spirit is a son of God. The spirit you received is not the spirit of slaves bringing fear into our lives again; it is the spirit of sons, and it makes us cry out, 'Abba, Father!' The Spirit himself and our spirit bear united witness that we are children of God. And if we are children we are heirs as well: heirs of God and co-heirs with Christ, sharing his sufferings so as to share his glory.

Romans 8: 14-17

When that day comes, over the House of David and the citizens of Jerusalem I will pour out a spirit of kindness and prayer. They will look upon the one they have pierced: they will mourn for him as for an only son, and weep for him as people weep for a first-born child.

Zechariah 12: 10

The love of Christ overwhelms us
when we reflect that if one has died for all,
then all men should be dead;
and the reason he died for all was so that living men
should live no longer for themselves,
but for him who died and was raised to life for them.

2 Corinthians 5: 14-15

I think that what we suffer in this life can never be compared to the glory,
as yet unrevealed, which is waiting for us.

Romans 8: 18

Think of what Christ suffered in this life, and then arm yourselves with the same resolution that he had: anyone who in this life has bodily suffering has broken with sin, because for the rest of his life on earth he is not ruled by human passions but only by the will of God.

1 Peter 4: 1-2

Remember, the ransom that was paid for you . . .
was not paid in anything corruptible, neither in silver or gold,
but in the precious blood of a lamb without stain,
namely Christ . . . Through him you now have faith in God,
who raised him from the dead and gave him glory
for that very reason –
so that you would have faith and hope in God.

1 Peter 1: 18-21

That day, you will say:
I give thanks to you, Yahweh . . .

He is the God of my salvation.
I have trust now and no fear,
for Yahweh is my strength, my song,
he is my salvation.
And you will draw water joyfully
from the springs of salvation.

Isaiah 12: 1-3

Though your body may be dead it is because of sin,
but if Christ is in you then your spirit is life itself
because you have been justified;
and if the Spirit of him who raised Jesus from the dead is living in you
then he who raised Jesus from the dead
will give life to your own mortal bodies through his Spirit living in you.

Romans 8: 10-11

JESUS IS LAID
IN THE TOMB
XIV

FOURTEENTH STATION

Jesus is laid in the Tomb

Pilate gave permission, so they came and took the body away. Nicodemus came as well – the same one who had first come to Jesus at night time – and he brought a mixture of myrrh and aloes, weighing about a hundred pounds. They took the body of Jesus and wrapped it with the spices in linen cloths, following the Jewish burial custom. At the place where he had been crucified there was a garden, and in this garden a new tomb in which no one had yet been buried. Since it was the Jewish Day of Preparation and the tomb was near at hand, they laid Jesus there.

John 19: 38-42

They gave him a grave with the wicked,
a tomb with the rich,
though he had done no wrong
and there had been no perjury in his mouth.
Yahweh had been pleased to crush him with suffering.

If he offers his life in atonement
he shall see his heirs, he shall have a long life
and through him what Yahweh wishes will be done.

Isaiah 53: 9-10

The wage paid by sin is death;
the present given by God is eternal life in Christ Jesus our Lord.

Romans 6: 23

You have been buried with him, when you were baptised:
and by baptism, too, you have been raised up with him
through your belief in the power of God
who raised him from the dead.
You were dead because you were sinners . . .
he has brought us to life with him,
he has forgiven us all our sins.

Colossians 2: 12-13

Fourteenth Station

Death where is your victory?
Death where is your sting?
Now the sting of death is sin, and sin gets its power from the Law.
So let us thank God for giving us victory
through our Lord Jesus Christ.

1 Corinthians 15: 55-57

When the kindness and love of God our Saviour for mankind were revealed, it was not because he was concerned with any righteous actions we might have done ourselves;

it was for no reason except his own compassion that he saved us, by means of the cleansing water of rebirth and by renewing us in the Holy Spirit which he so generously poured over us through Jesus Christ our saviour.

He did this so that we should be justified by his grace, to become heirs looking forward to inheriting eternal life.

Titus 3: 5-7

But God loves us with so much love
that he was generous with his mercy:

When we were dead through our sins,
he brought us to life with Christ
– it is through grace that you are saved –
and raised us up with him
and gave us a place with him in heaven,
in Christ Jesus.

Ephesians 2: 4-6

When we were baptised in Christ Jesus we were baptised in his death.
When we were baptised we went into the tomb with him
and joined him in death,
so that as Christ was raised from the dead by the Father's glory,
we too might live a new life.

Romans 6: 3-4

All I want to know is Christ and the power of his resurrection and to share in his sufferings by reproducing the pattern of his death. That is the way I can hope to take my place in the resurrection from the dead.

Philippians 3: 10-11

You have laid me in the depths of the tomb
in places that are dark, in the depths.
Imprisoned I cannot escape;
My eyes are sunken with grief.

I call to you Lord all the day long;
to you I stretch out my hands.

Psalm 87: 7, 9, 10

We must realise that our former selves
have been crucified with him
to destroy this sinful body and to free us from the slavery of sin.
When a man dies, of course, he has finished with sin.

Romans 6: 6-7

Lord, why do you reject me?
Why do you hide your face?
Friend and neighbour you have taken away
my one companion is darkness.

Psalm 87: 15, 19

But we believe that having died with Christ
we shall return to life with him:
Christ, as we know, having been raised from the dead
will never die again.

Death has no power over him any more.
When he died, he died once for all, to sin;
so his life now is life with God;

and in that way, you too must consider yourselves to be dead to sin
but alive for God in Christ Jesus.
For the wage paid by sin is death;
the present given by God is eternal life in Christ Jesus our Lord.

Romans 6: 8-11, 23

Fourteenth Station

Christ himself, innocent though he was, had died once for sins,
died for the guilty, to lead us to God.
In the body he was put to death, in the spirit he was raised to life,
and in the spirit, he went to preach to the spirits in prison.

1 Peter 3: 18-19

Because he is their judge, too,
the dead had to be told the good news as well.

1 Peter 4: 6

I think that what we suffer in this life can never be compared to the glory, as yet unrevealed, which is waiting for us.

From the beginning till now
the entire creation has been groaning in one great act of giving birth:
and not only creation, but all of us who possess the first fruits of the Spirit,
we too groan inwardly as we wait for our bodies to be set free.
For we must be content to hope that we shall be saved.

Romans 8: 18, 22-24

With God on our side, who can be against us?

Since God did not spare his only Son, but gave him up to benefit us all,
we may be certain, after such a gift,
that he will not refuse us anything he can give.

He not only died for us – he rose from the dead,
and there at God's right hand he stands and pleads for us.

Nothing, therefore, can come between us and the love of Christ,
even if we are troubled or worried, or being persecuted,
or lacking food and clothes, or being threatened, or even attacked.
These are the trials through which we triumph,
by the power of him who loved us.

For I am certain of this: neither death nor life, no angel,
no prince, nothing that exists, nothing still to come,
not any power or height or depth, or any created thing,
can ever come between us and the love of God
made visible in Christ Jesus our Lord.

Romans 8: 31, 32, 34-35, 37-39

That day,
I will make the sun go down at noon,
and darken the earth in broad daylight.
I will make it a mourning like the mourning for an only son,
as long as it lasts it will be like a day of bitterness.

Amos 8: 9-10

For my soul is filled with evils;
my life is on the brink of the grave.
I am reckoned as one in the tomb:
I have reached the end of my strength.

Like one alone among the dead;
like the slain lying in their graves;
like those you remember no more
cut off as they are from your hand.

Psalm 87: 4-7

I keep the Lord ever in my sight:
since he is at my right hand, I shall stand firm.

And so my heart rejoices, my soul is glad;
even my body shall rest in safety.
For you will not leave my soul among the dead,
nor let your beloved know decay.

You will show me the path of life,
the fulness of joy in your presence,
at your right hand happiness for ever.

Psalm 15: 8-11

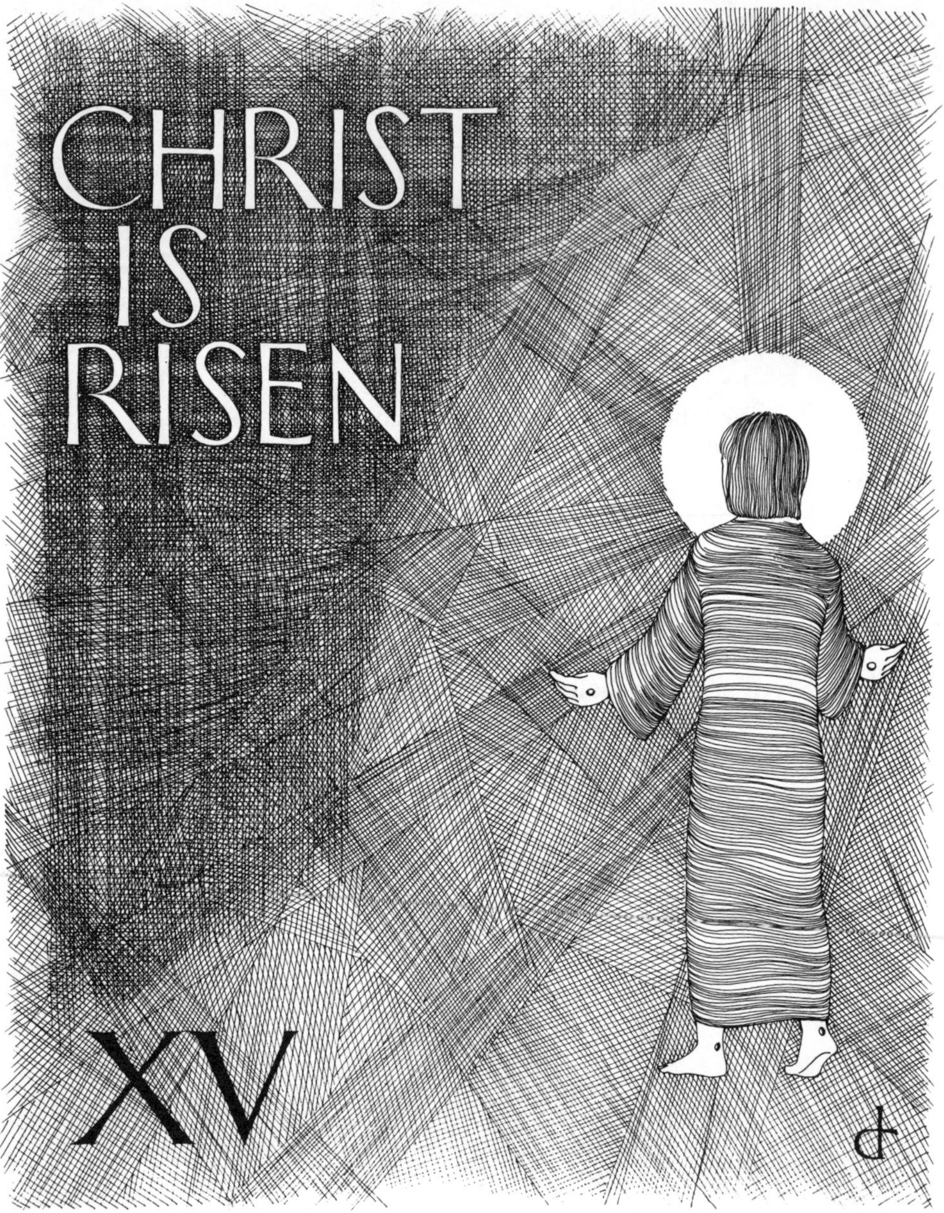

CHRIST IS RISEN

XV

FIFTEENTH STATION

Christ is risen

Alleluia!

Praise God in his holy place,
praise him in his mighty heavens.
Praise him for his powerful deeds,
praise his surpassing greatness.

O praise him with the sound of trumpet,
praise him with lute and harp.
Praise him with timbrel and dance,
praise him with strings and pipes.

O praise him with resounding cymbals,
praise him with the clashing of cymbals.
Let everything that lives and breathes
give praise to the Lord.

Alleluia!

Psalm 150

I am the resurrection.
If anyone believes in me, even though he dies he will live,
and whoever lives and believes in me
will never die.

Do you believe this?

John 11: 25-26

I am the Way, the Truth and the Life.
If you know me you know my Father, too.

John 14: 7

We know that the son of God has come,
and has given us the power to know the true God.

We are in the true God as we are in his Son, Jesus Christ.

This is the true God, this is eternal life.

1 John 5: 20

Fifteenth Station

That very day, two of the disciples were on their way to a village called Emmaus, seven miles from Jerusalem, and they were talking together about all that had happened. Now as they talked this over, Jesus himself came up and walked by their side; but something prevented them from recognising him. He said to them, 'What matters are you discussing as you walk along?' They stopped short, their faces downcast . . . 'All about Jesus of Nazareth,' they answered' 'who proved he was a great prophet by the things he said and did in the sight of God and of the whole people; and our chief priests and our leaders handed him over to be sentenced to death, and had him crucified. Our hope had been that he would be the one to set Israel free' . . . Then he said to them, 'You foolish men! So slow to believe the full message of the prophets! Was it not ordained that Christ should suffer and so enter into his glory?' Then, starting with Moses and going through all the prophets, he explained the passages throughout the scriptures that were about himself . . . They pressed him to stay with them . . . Now while he was with them at table, he took the bread and said the blessing; then he broke it and handed it to them. And their eyes were opened and they recognised him; but he vanished from their sight.

Luke 24: 13-17, 19-20, 25-30

Epilogue

This, then, is what I pray, kneeling before the Father:
Out of his infinite glory,
may he give you the power through his Spirit
for your hidden self to grow strong,
so that Christ may live in your heart through Faith,
and then, planted in love and built on love,
you will with all the saints
have the strength to grasp
the breadth and length, the height and depth;
until,
knowing the love of Christ, which is beyond all knowledge,
you are filled with the utter fulness of God.

Glory be to him, whose power, working in us
can do infinitely more than we ask or imagine;
Glory be to him
from generation to generation in the church
and in Christ Jesus for ever and ever.

Amen.

Ephesians 3: 16-21